The Rivers Keep Singing

poems by

ALEXANDRA CRIVICI-KRAMER

Testimonials

"This is a rare creation of song and scar, of vulnerability and eco-consciousness, of emotional complexity and simple witness. In Alexandra Crivici-Kramer's new collection *The Rivers Keep Singing*, the natural and human worlds mingle in accessible, personal, yet almost mythic ways. From lush to bare, the landscapes she presents us with are so intertwined with and impacted by our actions that we realize the two have always been one. Brimming with meditations deep as winter snow and boundless compassion and curiosity, these vibrant poems remain grounded in a universal familiarity that opens us up to something greater. If one of the aims of poetry is to condense our vast, contradictory, and beautiful world into the briefest of songs, *The Rivers Keep Singing* stands as a testament to its possibility."

— John Sibley Williams author of *As One Fire Consumes Another*.

"This poetry moves my soul back into the forest and washes my heart in all the rivers my body can remember. Alexandra's tone and relationship with the trees, the water, and the earth echo on each page, on a deep cellular level. She reminds me of what it means to be alive. To be human - without all the noise. The beautiful silence of nature and existence"

— Jamie Nix, Poet & Agroforestry Scientist

The Rivers Keep Singing

Acknowledgements:

I must first thank my parents who have grounded me and supported me from the beginning.

Thank you to my professors and the community at the Bread Loaf School of English, your teaching and wisdom is something I will always carry.

Thank you to my students— I have learned more from you than you'll ever know.

And to my three greatest loves:

Jack— thank you for always pouring your light when I need it most.
Wilder & Brooks— my most wild miracles.
Vermont— this beautiful place I call home, thank you, thank you, thank you.

Table of Contents

An Invitation   7

¤ **In the Company of Trees** ¤   8

Mornings   9
A Two-Dimensional Reverie   10
Family Recipe   11
In The Company of Trees   12
Camouflage   13
Splitting   14
Roots   15
White Dress   16
Jane Doe   17
Endangered Species   18
Al Dente   19
The Bite   20
Stick Season   21

¤ **I Know These Woods** ¤   22

As Above So Below   23
November   24
Snow Had Fallen   25
Stillness   26
Winter Blues   27
Forest Music   28
Wandering   29
Vermont   30
Together We Are Sovereign   31
Unapologetic   32
The Lesson   33-34
This One is for the Trees   35
Postpartum   36
I Know These Woods   37

¤ **Stay Awhile** ¤   38

Thoughts of Spring   39
Rising   40
Our Breath Like Prayers   41
Stay Awhile   42
Deliverance   43
Wild River   44
Praying   45
Welcome Home   46
The Body as a River   47
Practical Wisdom   48
June   49
Wild Knowing   50
Ode to Sand   51
You Bring Out the Dirt Roads in Me   52-53
Due Date   54
Resilience   55
Sunrise   56
October in New England   57
Cycle Breaker   58

¤ **Wild with Gratitude** ¤   60

"I'd been to the river before, a few times.
Don't blame the river that nothing happened quickly.
You don't hear such voices in an hour or a day.
You don't hear them at all if selfhood has stuffed your ears."

–Mary Oliver: At the River Clarion

"It is a wholesome and necessary thing for us to turn again to the earth and in the contemplation of her beauties to know the sense of wonder and humility."

–Rachel Carson

An Invitation

Come as you are into the woods,
leave your clothes & shoes behind.
Get down on hands & knees, like back
when we all howled & thrashed &
bled as one pack of wild

knowing. Remember how
we chewed & mouthed what it means
to be alive? Remember when our eyes
were filled with fire?

¤

In the Company of Trees

¤

Mornings

I wake with the sun
so that I can witness

the light dance
across the skin

of rivers,
and the darkness

creep
back into the woods

like a wounded shadow.

These woods are thick
with truths

I have not yet
learned

to name.

**A Two-Dimensional Reverie
Subject of the *Mona Lisa:***

Muddy creeks & trees leaking greens unfurl
behind me.

My eyes, full of concrete knowing:
loss & joy are two separate pillars, yet

grief is a watercolor, deceptive
like an upturned mouth.

Would I rather breathe in those muted blues,
mourning the death of my child?

Or with cheeks flushed & hair
wild, knotted with inky leaves
from an afternoon romp with a man,
who is not my husband,

so that I can sit here, unflinching,
serene for the painter's gaze?

Or is it everything
everything
all at once?

Family Recipe

I am from where mountains meet oceans & rust mixes
with mineral muck at the base of rivers, stuck

between toes painted red like the sauce I ate
on Sundays & the red that gushed

between these legs after my 11th time circling the sun,
to whom I pray to now that *the blood won't come,*

a prayer passed down

by my mother, grandmother, & great grandmother
while gripping a wooden spoon in dim kitchen light.

In the Company of Trees

Leafless trees cast spells with naked hands.
Palms press a sky filled with ghosts.
Our breath, like smoke will rise,
as truth escapes

the body.

Camouflage

I am a curator of grief.

I like to hide myself
in tall trees.

I am a collector
of wild words

clips of rivers &
snapshots of mountains.

I like
to feel humbled

by blue sky
that will outlive me.

Splitting

It started   with a fissure
the tearing   of tissue
more than   a before
& after, more like how
lightning   strikes wood,
splinters   into flesh,
obliterates,   a body.
Broken.   Erased.

Ashes,   then a woman

      Wild.

Roots

How much history needs
searching
to find not the rib,
but the root?
That first tree
where she plucked
the finest fruit
took a bite &

filled herself with sweetest knowing?

I want to return
to that moment &
help her consume
everything to the core,
then sow the seeds &
save some for winter. Can
you imagine if every woman
tasted such abundance?

White Dress

Picture me in the trees, clutching
a bouquet of weeds, holding
onto a singular belief, praying
nature will fix me.

Like a bird I am prisoner
inside my head, caged
by the violence
on that bed, tethered
to this body, *I wish I were dead.*
    But I walk into the woods
    instead.

If I marry the earth
would I be cleansed? If
I give myself to these trees
could they mend
this shame? Or
maybe just maybe
help me

transcend.

Jane Doe

Flashes of brown leap
across flecked
white

screech, halt
crunch, teeth
on bone

knees crouch
beside wounded fur,
earth a muddy red

brown eyes search,
Run
they said.

Endangered Species

The last Vermont Catamount was shot in 1881 on
Thanksgiving Day.

These cats enjoyed deer, the occasional sheep,
and like me, liked to hide in forests of tall trees.

Those trees— slaughtered, became farms.
What happens when home is changed

without consent? Privilege allows some to leave,
pack a bag or fly south. But most

will fight,
before becoming
a fossil of this landscape.

Preserved behind glass, pay ten cents
to gawk, take field trips to learn about

how the world is always evolving.

This is how they made their dens,
This is how they cared for their young.

This is how those in power have always
changed the story.

Al Dente

We Italians say that
the undercooked pasta
floating at the top
of the pot
is perfection.
Al Dente
we crunch
with our teeth
like moonless wolves.

Maybe we are in a hurry;
maybe we see the still—
raw stalk suspended
in the salted water
as a metaphor.
Or maybe
we have learned to bite
anything that makes us feel wild.

The Bite

White teeth pierced my flesh before my gums were fully healed from my perpetual prodding. I remember time slowing down, limbs moving through honey, my own breathing, louder than the desperate bite of a rabid dog. I feared the hush of my mother's voice. So I never cried out, never screamed, just waited for the bleeding to stop. *That was where I learned to stay mute.* At 19 I remember my own heartbeat was the loudest sound in the room, time was in retrograde and suddenly I was that little girl afraid to scream. He obliterated me into an almost nothing. Days were long but nights were cosmic. I slept. Started charting the moon's dance. Stopped hacking away parts of what made me wild. I became wild. Now I am consumed with the visceral need to sink my sharp, white teeth into his skin. And howl.

Stick Season

Slant light shatters on a forest floor
hidden by leaves that will decay
before our next heartbreak.

Oh how fragile it all seems,
this cycling of seasons, this
growth we all endure.

I want to breathe in
that place where time is still,
where a moment can be

absorbed,
enjoyed,
slipped beneath our
tongues.

I Know These Woods

As Above, So Below

Behind our house a fox sniffs gray air.
She noses the wind with precise inflection, urgent
to discover food that she will not eat —
just one of her daily sacrifices.
Persistent, her head bends low to the ground —
prayers made of dirt
and grass.

I too am stuck between
the role of mother
the role of myself.

November

Now the season of sticks, naked gray smoke.

Leafless trees cast long shadows, illuminating
half-moons around my weathered eyes.

Nobody knows
the trouble I've seen

But you just never saw me when
that sparse golden light

shatters & sometimes
I forget the space between

my bones, dry
as the wood I gave for your fire.

Nobody knows my sorrow

I want to slumber
under blankets lined with soft snow,

until I muster strength
to rise again

Glory Hallelujah

Snow Had Fallen

Snow had fallen
Snow on snow on snow
In the bleak midwinter
          — Christina Rossetti

In a New England Wood
naked maple and oak trees stand vigil
like the dark shadows of late January.

Snow clings to their boughs and
bark like a stubborn memory.
I've forgotten
how these giant plants see
without the guise of winter.

Sometimes this wonder of mine
leaves me dizzy, and helpless, and
alone. Surrounded by nothing
but snow on snow on snow.

Still, a cluster of birch trees
with their young faces and
open palms release
the myth of this season.
They raise delicate arms
to a blank sky, and bend
towards the light.

Stillness

When the river of our minds stills
we hear the silence within.
Every corner, a warm fire
in a wood cabin in December.
Tufts of snow drift
as rivers begin to freeze.

This is more than your grief.
Listen for the least sound —
the snap of a twig,
evergreens groan
under their white winter weight.

When has a river been judged
by the speed of its water, rather
than its meandering path,
or ability to cut
through rock?

This temporal death of all things
knows that silence does not keep. It
exhales. Breathing back into earth,
into us.

Winter Blues

I long for the precariousness
of a winter's day.
When cobalt blue pops
against a stark white —
almost as harrowing
as a single drop of blood
in clear water, like some primordial
creature of the sea.

Tentacles stretch,
        pirouette,
                and spread
                        until the water
                blushes,
        ensconced
with just this

moment.

Days of January sometimes clump together
until that one short day, sky brilliant, sun shy
easing monotony and teasing a moment of magic
in a world where I have almost lost hope.

Forest Music

Each tree creates millions
of opportunities for music.
Notice how each branch
moves like a poem.
Notice each undulation,
each small click, creak,
and groan,
the percussion of winter,
like bone
on bone.

Do you also wander
a forest alone like a wolf?
Rumi suggests to be held
we must open our hands.
Or maybe learn
from these trees
who flourish
in always widening
rings of being.

Wandering

I too play at the edges of knowing.
I walk riverbanks in pale pink morning,
leave my boots muddy
at the door to places
I never fully call home.

I do not feel the need to carve
my initials into this landscape,
I pray for impermanence.

    A snowflake poised
    on my son's pink nose,
    melts into poreless skin.
    His eyes wide,

        amazed.

Vermont

It is not a lecture.
It is not here to teach us
of death. It hasn't the time
for such pontification.

To stand rooted to our truest selves
— our most naked selves,
takes courage.

A Maple Tree
surrounded by a memory
of its Autumn beauty.

Vermont makes me feel
like I am in the company of God —
a love so persistent despite temporality.
In rivers flowing and under
mountains of brown leaves I find
belonging.

Together We Are Sovereign

Not enough.

It's what we've inherited,
what we've always heard,
and what we've learned to say
when words struggled
to find their meaning.

We feigned our humanity & always
stayed close to the ground.
Survived off the dirt
we've been fed, became
comfortable with emptiness.

But how can we see
ourselves, each other, with chins
tucked, hands & knees
bloody?

Great cats also creep low
to the earth, but they know
how to get what they want.
Together they circle prey,
together they sink their teeth, and
together they are sovereign

Unapologetic

After Sonya Renee Taylor

A birch tree stands alone, ensconced
by ribbons of white bark —
a luxuriant queen, now in rags,
like some relic of folklore.

I press my ear to her skin and
she whispers,
the body is not an apology.
I take this as an invitation
to stand bare with her—

two women,
proud in our nakedness

The Lesson

When the haze lifted and my body became only mine again,
I spent our days wandering while you mostly slept.
As we strolled, I took in our new world

The lake, long and silvering, a meadow
wild with oxeye daisies, then later
yellowing grass and a great oak tree

with golden leaves held tightly like my hands
gripping the handlebar, or my heart gripping
memories from before I became your mother.

One day, in mid March the lake was a still life,
& the meadow, a dense slate of white.
I assumed the oak would be a similar

picture of winter, or maybe even dead.
Yet there it was, filled with an exaltation
of red-breasted robins. They flitted from branch

to branch, amass of wonder, and feathers,
greeting one another after months of solitude.
When was the last time I felt such joy?

Would I chirp or sing upon seeing a familiar face?
Have I grown so familiar with emptiness,
where I was once filled with life?

Yet there you were,
the life I grew, wild
as the glinted lake,
a summer meadow,
and now this tree —
bursting with hope.

Your coos and squeals
as if to tell them:
Here I am!
Here you are!
I am so glad to see you!
And on that day, you taught me
how our truest nature
is that of wonder,
is that of warmth.

This One is for the Trees

living on the banks of rivers
      black tupelo,
      weeping willow,
      red maple,
      river birch

just to name a few.
I wonder if these trees grow weary
or wish they could uproot &
meet a friend for coffee (or a drink?)
or maybe just close their eyes and sleep.
Do you see their roots caked in mud, &
their bloated, heavy limbs?
Do you see their outstretched branches
creating shade, creating safety?
Do you smell the exhaustion in their skin?

This one is for the mothers
whose
      children
           move
                like rivers,
         this way
& that,
      constantly.

Fearlessly.

Your love allows
the rivers to stay wild.

For this I celebrate you.
For this I thank you.

Postpartum

The foliage came late this year. What usually ends
in October stretched until that season, when I
move slowly and finally notice my breath. Am I
so selfish to think that it was for me? To see the
birch hold onto its golden cloak a little longer
until a conflagration took hold of the forest? Even
when the wind wanted attention the trees held
tightly to their leaves, like a new mother holds her
baby — incredulous that anyone allowed her to
take on this role. As I stare at my child, my heart
is on fire, and the trees mirror it back to me.

I thank them for this reflection.

I Know These Woods

Just as I know the soft and spiraling
vowels of my mother's voice
pushing up through the earth
like fiddleheads in June.

That my father's steps
smell of sun
yearned by thawing soil.

And my grandmother's hands —
a map, each blue vein —
a root system of history
and hope.

Just like I know
the robin's song,
the coyote's wail, the groan
of wind in these very branches

like lovers in the naked bloom of morning,

I know these woods like my own name.
And how delicious it sounds inside your mouth.

¤

Stay Awhile

¤

Thoughts of Spring

Hope is still
the thing feathered, that perches
on the feeder outside your window.

Be still and know
that unexpected comfort
in a February snow
is something we all
need to survive. Be

still and know
that gratitude is heard best when

silent. Listen

to that embodied hum,
flutter of wings, and know
you are the witness
of joy.

Rising

I've thought about all of the mundane
& creative ways to stop breathing.

To come as close as a stone's throw, to peer
beyond

life's steep, sloping precipice and
finally reach a satisfying exhale.

Or perhaps
leap

accept gravity,
grow feathers,

& see fields of dark
red poppies

trees birthing a nation
of humble green.

My god, this life is beautiful!
I thunder to the sun.

Our Breath Like Prayers

Imagine if we greeted each morning
with the grace of an open hand?
Our breath hangs in the air
like a promise
reminding us
to be with what is,
to be here now.

Stay Awhile

*"Around me the trees stir in their leaves
and call out, stay awhile."*
— **Mary Oliver**

She went to the mountains,
learned to forage, to trust

rivers, meandered through
wild grass, studied still waters

built a home of bark,
and brambles, and elderberry, peeled back

layer upon layer of this green earth, revealing
dirt, roots, her pulsing heart.

Deliverance

The minutes before I became a mother
was the closest I have ever been to something truly
wild.

My heart rapid like the river
after rain,
fluid & focused & raw.
Incessant — almost holy.
I was out of body,

out of mind, and completely
at the mercy of nature.

I became
nature.
Brought arms
between legs
& became
my own wild
miracle.

Wild River

Oh, I've known you wild
    wild river. Your sneaky curves
        and silky banks. I know your seasons,
          your parched thirsty skin,
      shallow and thin,
    waiting for the rains to come again
turning back time making you
    buoyant and full of want. I've seen you
        galloping south to north
       you cut through mountains of green
    and white, ancient granite holding
memories from when we were water.

Praying

May your tongue
be infinite

in the many apologies
it learns to utter. May

you unlearn the habit
of biting down, seething,

growling towards
the foreign terrain you see

in the mirror.

Welcome Home

As a child I learned to seek
acceptance outside of the body.
As if these limbs, bones,
flesh & heart so filled with fire
was not enough.

I invented such wild realities
under the protection of evergreens,
fashioned sanctuaries out of their
snowlined wombs.
Shame & pressed leaves
crowded my pockets.
I collected accolades like rocks,
Maybe now they will love me,
which really meant, *maybe now
I will love me.*

I called this ambition the trait I inherited,
*immigrant descendant, not made
of this soil,* I needed to prove my
belonging. But I have bled into this place,
left my heart all over this state,
this home that accepted me.
Now each day I try to accept
this body,
this home.

The Body as a River

I remember when I learned my body
is a river. In some places a whisper,

& in others louder than the groans
of a cut tree.

Clear, roiled, demure, expansive.

Fed by rain, adored by roots
of ferns. In late summer

wildflowers bloom along
my edges, & in winter I learn to

live beneath
the superficial.

I can hold a landscape
on my hip, a valley

in the crook of my arm —
safe, swaddled, and warm.

Oh how free I felt,

when I welcomed
impermanence

and gave this body
the grace to transform

Practical Wisdom

Let me keep
        my distance, away
                from those who think
                        they have the answers. Away

from the news of bombs,
        of blood; find comfort
                under the pines, where still,
                        life has some possibility

left, and God is surely listening.
        I don't know where prayers
                go, I only know that the rivers
                        keep singing.

I too have known
        what it is to feel misunderstood,
                rejected, and suddenly not at all
                        beautiful.

But there is a fire
        in the lashes of my eyes,
                and the rivers are still
                        singing. This world

is not just a little thrill,
        all that glorious
                temporary stuff. Beauty exists
                        and sometimes I need to stand

wherever I am to be blessed,
        the shore, the woods, the mountains.
                        What I am trying to say is:
                                Love yourself.

                        Then forget it.

June

It's after the rains, after
the flood, after
the mud has dried &
nothing but dust
& bone remain, after
night turns to light &
purple sky mates
with mountains green
like a healing bruise, when sand
stops passing through the glass,
where you finally pause &
breathe.

Wild Knowing

I remember your face when I said yes
& our palms became one, electric

when you traced my edges
& consumed me with eyes

overflowing with blue. I've imagined
every moment, lived it twice.

Each day was as long as a lifetime.

I know this to be true because I have lived
a thousand different versions of myself.

My soul has witnessed every rain
every phase of desperation &

I have been waiting
to say *yes*.

Even when this fleshy cage
shatters

I will still be everlasting.

Ode to Sand

I love the way you linger
in the places of my body

that cannot be shaken out.
That   slow   magic

delicate strokes blending
earth, ocean, & flesh

smoothing the edges
between   worlds.

You make me want to lay
down on that inherited

daisied sheet & muse
the kingdom between

what is mythic
& what is concrete.

You Bring Out the Dirt Roads in Me
After Sandra Cisneros

You bring out the dirt road in me.
The winding, uncharted turns in me.
The hard packed earth —
smells delicious after the rain.
You bring out the wild river in me.
I'd flood a whole town and take the bridges with me.
    For you, yes.
    For you.
You bring out the small town in me.
The radical white-haired politician in me.
The fire on the mountain in October.
The yellow barn and the bumble bee.
The melancholic song of the loon.
You bring out the crispness of November nights in me.
I am the glow of a wood stove.
    Baby, I can keep you warm.
    Oh, yes. I can.
You bring out the wine stained sky in me.
The flannel-lined inebriation in me.
You bring out the funk in me.
The playful boogie of bluegrass.
Hips sway like the limbs of the
Maple Sugar Tree.
    You like it.
    Yes, you do.

You bring out the wanderer in me.
The howl of winter.
The drive all night to see you,
in me.
You bring out the wife in me.
The *Let's grow roots and stay forever*
in these mountains —
the first place I called home.
But you bring out the *home* in me.
You are the only one
I'd leave these dirt roads for.
I'd trade them for traffic,
so much traffic,
concrete, and the Golden Gate Bridge.
  For you. Oh yes.
  I would.

Due Date

Time was amorphous
between states like honey on the tongue,
not quite liquid
but enough to sweeten
the opaque uncertainty swarming
my belly
swollen as if stung.
To be present in this body
takes my full effort, not
as instinctual as I'd hoped.
Where are the low groans
my ancestors moaned in squats
so deep their bodies became the earth
I now pace?
My budding hips
too wide to romanticize
or feminize — they have a job to do.
They don't need your flattery or verbal slimming.
Let me feel expansive —
a full moon looming over a blue ocean — a woman
bearing down, adding to her legacy.

Resilience

Which is fiercer,
mountains or clouds?

Mountains are immovable
capable of terrible things.

But oh, how the wisps of water gather,
bring relief to parched roots &
fear to bloated bellies of boats. To hold so much
in arms soft as mounds of dough,
but know when to let go,
to untether
what is heavy.

Dare the mountains not to crumble,
remind them what you carry.

Sunrise
For Wilder

This is where the waiting ends.

Where the pink and indigo of in between becomes
blue sky and golden sun. Oh the sun,
oh the sun, with imperial knowing
even in this beginning.

Where only the music of machines and
whoosh whoosh of hearts — yours and mine,
pierced the heaviness of a room saturated
with breaths held
like a prayer.

Where thought becomes action,
action becomes noun —
a breathing, and bleeding, and
beautiful noun.

Oh, my son
Oh, my son.

This is where we begin.

October in New England

I feel the most beautiful
in this golden light, caught
between green & naked,
alive & dead.

This moment of reverence:
a hawk wing blurs blue air,
& God is all around me.

Cycle Breaker
for my children

You do not have to carry these burdens
you've inherited

You do not have to believe
what you've been trained to believe.

You can strip,
expose your shadowed skin and
leap

into water a clear blue, find yourself
on a mountain of green

slice the sky
like the black wing of a great bird

and live as boldly
as your ancestors
dreamed.

Wild With Gratitude

The last of the November geese fly
in muddy morning light, and I am
caught in the middle of rooted
and wild.

I don't know what the soft
animal of my body desires,
and I worry I am out of time.
Maybe I too should leave this place
before winter freezes everything and
I am made part of these mountains.

Sometimes I wonder
if I was built to endure
this kind of hardening —
how easily the bones
get cold, how easily
I become embittered.

But then out of the flat light
a yellow sun blooms and births
a crimson sky. Slate mountains
bow before this daily miracle,
as the last black wings
glide south.

Cold air undresses
my held breath,
and I am both lost and found,

I am home.

ABOUT THE POET
ALEXANDRA CRIVICI-KRAMER

Alexandra learned at a young age how vital the natural world is in shaping who we are. Although Vermont has not always been her address, she has never felt more at home in a place — it is where her poetry lives.

Alexandra is a member of the Poetry Society of Vermont and is a graduate from The University of Vermont, and The Bread Loaf School of English at Middlebury College.

Her poetry can be found in *The Mountain Troubadour, The Bread Loaf Journal, The Inflectionist Review, The Button Eye Review, SWWIM,* and *The Middlebury Centennial Journal* among others. Alexandra is also the winner of the 2022 International Merit Award in the *Atlanta Review.* She lives in Shelburne, Vermont with her husband, dog, and two sons where she can be found walking in the woods or swimming in the rivers, with a notebook never too far away.

ABOUT THE PUBLISHER
PLANTS & POETRY

Plants & Poetry is a small, women- and indigenous-owned business founded in Northwest Arkansas in 2019. Cofounders Jamie Nix and Leslie Walker create a space that nurtures a love for the arts and science, offering poetry & plant education to reconnect with the soil and soul.

Plants & Poetry is a small organization on a mission to bridge the arts and science to inspire communities to reconnect with the environment. To cultivate this bridge, the organization has created a nature-inspired literary journal, *Plants & Poetry Journal*, and a community food forest, The Oasis, in Bella Vista, AR.

www.plantsandpoetry.org

www.plantsandpoetry.org